Twisting Up a Storm

Cheryl Duksta

Learning Media

Contents

1. Something Strange in the Air

Dark, heavy clouds hung in the sky above central Texas on 27 May 1997. People reported that "something strange was in the air" all day. Late that afternoon, a severe storm began, and the local TV stations issued tornado warnings.

In the small town of Jarrell, Texas, a nine-year-old girl called Kristen was watching the clouds with her mother when they saw that a tornado was heading toward them. They hurried inside, got in the bathtub, and pulled cushions over their heads. The last thing they heard was the roof being ripped off their house, then they were hurled through the air. The next thing Kristen remembers is waking up beside a tree. She looked up and saw her mother in the branches. Her mother couldn't call for help because her lungs were filled with dirt and dust. Kristin and her mother had serious injuries, but they survived.

The Jarrell tornado killed twenty-seven people on that terrible day, including Kristen's father, who had been lying beside them on the bathroom floor. The tornado's winds blew at over 260 miles per hour, completely wiping homes from their concrete slabs and sucking the pavement off roads. Most of the buildings in the town were destroyed. Very few people in the direct path of the tornado survived.

About a thousand tornadoes (often called twisters) occur in the United States every year. Most happen in spring, when the weather is **humid**. They are especially frequent in the area known as Tornado Alley, which runs from Texas in the south to Canada in the north.

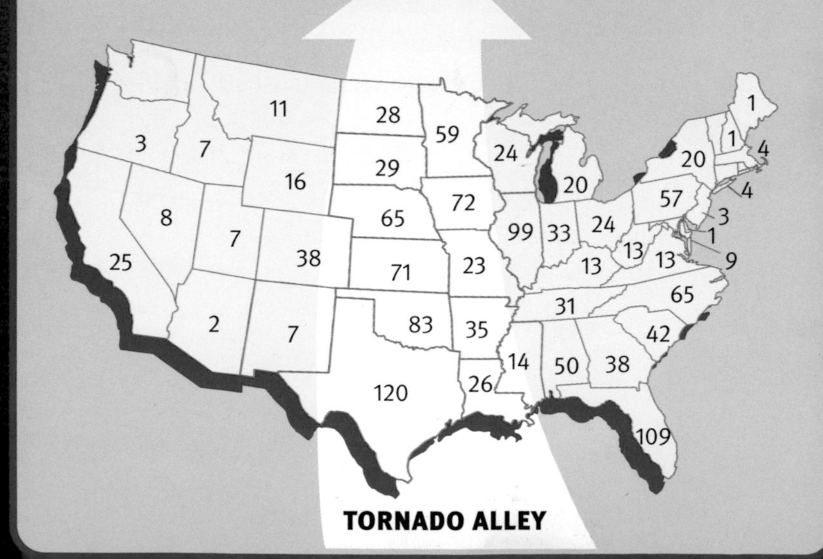

Tornado Facts

- The United States has more tornadoes than any other country in the world.
- In May, the peak month for tornadoes, there can be as many as five a day.
- In 1974, 148 tornadoes ripped through thirteen states over a 12-hour period.
- Only 5–10% of storms produce a tornado.
- Sometimes a large tornado is surrounded by smaller tornadoes that are very powerful even though they may be less than 10 feet wide.
- Some tornadoes are very narrow, and their path of destruction can be very clearly defined. For example, a tornado might completely destroy one house but leave its neighbor untouched.
- Most tornadoes last less than 10 minutes, and seldom travel more than 25 miles.

Tri-State Tornado

The most devastating tornado in American history was the Tri-State Tornado, which ripped across Missouri, Illinois, and Indiana in 1925, completely destroying four towns and killing 689 people. The tornado traveled for 219 miles and lasted almost 4 hours.

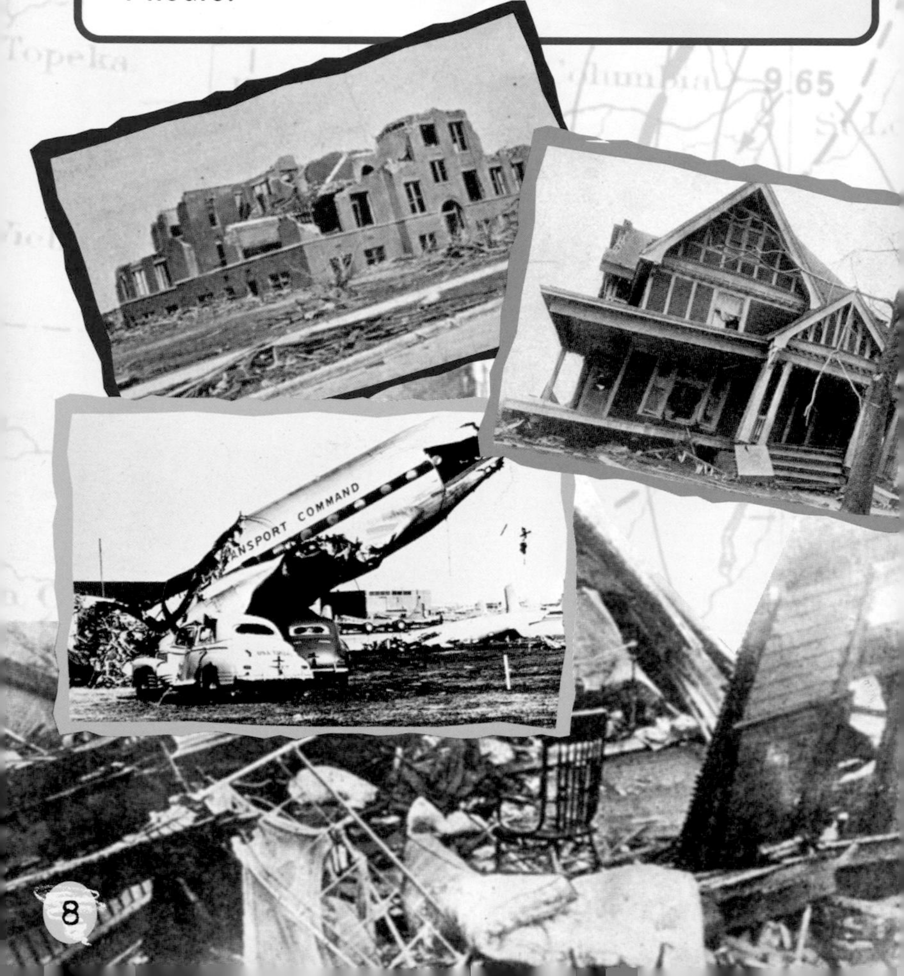

2. The Path of Destruction

Tornadoes are rated not by their size but by the amount of damage they cause. The damage usually depends on the strength of the tornado's winds.

Scientist Ted Fujita developed a rating system called the Fujita Scale that has six levels, F0 to F5. The Jarrell tornado was an F5 – one of the worst tornadoes ever.

Fujita Tornado Intensity Scale

F0
40–72 miles per hour

Light Damage – damages chimneys, breaks tree branches

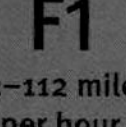

F1
73–112 miles per hour

Moderate Damage – overturns mobile homes, moves cars

F2
113–157 miles per hour

Significant Damage – tears roofs off houses, destroys mobile homes, uproots trees

F3
158–206 miles per hour

Severe Damage – overturns trains, throws cars

F4
207–260 miles per hour

Devastating Damage – levels well-built houses, turns big objects into flying missiles

F5
261–318 miles per hour

Incredible Damage – lifts houses and carries them some distance, throws cars through the air

40 60 80 100 120 140 160 180 200 220 240 260 280 300 32

wind speed (miles per hour)

Picking Up the Pieces

After a tornado has hit, it can take a long time for life to return to normal. The injured must be treated and homes and community facilities rebuilt. After the Jarrell tornado, a center was set up at the local school for people who had lost their homes, and community groups and construction companies helped with the rebuilding work.

Weird Tornado Damage

After a tornado, there are always amazing stories told of its awesome power. For example, there are people who claim to have seen:

- a vinyl record driven into a telephone pole
- chickens found alive, totally plucked of their feathers
- a store wall completely destroyed, but a shelf that stood against it left untouched
- a whole pond of fish sucked up and then "rained" down – still alive
- five horses that were picked up by a tornado in Kansas found a quarter of a mile away, unhurt, still hitched to the same rail
- an iron jug blown inside out!

3. Twisting Up a Storm

Tornadoes are difficult to study because no one ever knows for sure when or where one may happen, and even if you find one, it's dangerous to get close. So **meteorologists** still have a lot of unanswered questions about exactly how tornadoes form. They think that the process is something like this:

1. A storm begins to form when cold, dry air meets warm, wet air. The boundary between the two air masses is called a front.

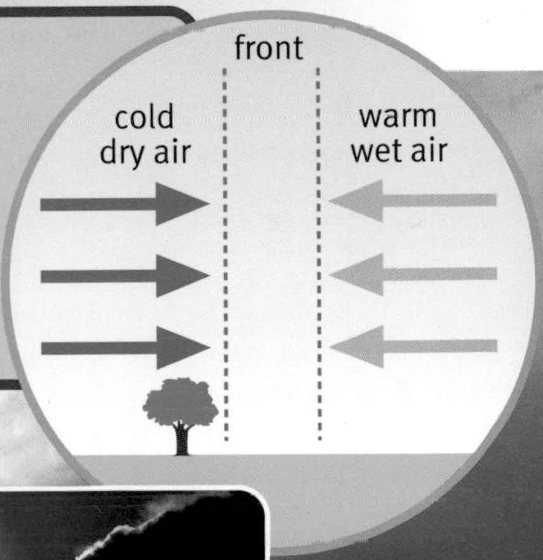

front
cold dry air
warm wet air

2. When the warm and cold air meet, the cold air pushes the warm air up. As the air rises, clouds form. These clouds can get very big and become thunderclouds that may produce lightning, thunder, and heavy rain.

3. In order for a tornado to form, the thundercloud must rotate or turn. This will happen if air blowing from another direction bumps into it. Then the cloud will begin turning around and down like a corkscrew. A storm that has begun to rotate is called a supercell. Supercell storms are the main producers of tornadoes.

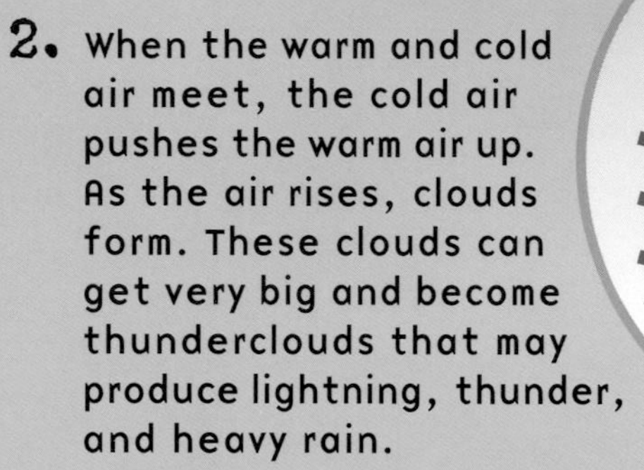

4. The rotating air may form a funnel-shaped cloud that begins to drop down from the supercell. (Not all supercells produce **funnel clouds**.) A funnel cloud is harmless if it just spins in the air and doesn't touch trees, buildings, or the ground. But if the funnel cloud does reach the ground, it becomes a tornado.

5. When the funnel cloud hits the ground, it begins stirring up dirt, dust, and debris, which make the tornado become darker and easier to see.

A tornado that touches a lake or the sea sucks up the water and forms a waterspout.

6. A tornado can survive as long as it has energy to keep spinning. For a tornado to lose its energy, it must be overcome by a strong force of air that cuts off the tornado's energy source so that the tornado "dies." A dying tornado sometimes looks like a thin rope floating back into the sky.

4. Tracking Tornadoes

Meteorologists make use of various tools to forecast and track storms. As the technology keeps improving, they will be able to learn more about tornadoes and so help people avoid or survive them.

Weather Balloons

Meteorologists use weather balloons to collect and record information about air temperature, air pressure, and humidity. This helps them predict when and where storms and tornadoes may happen.

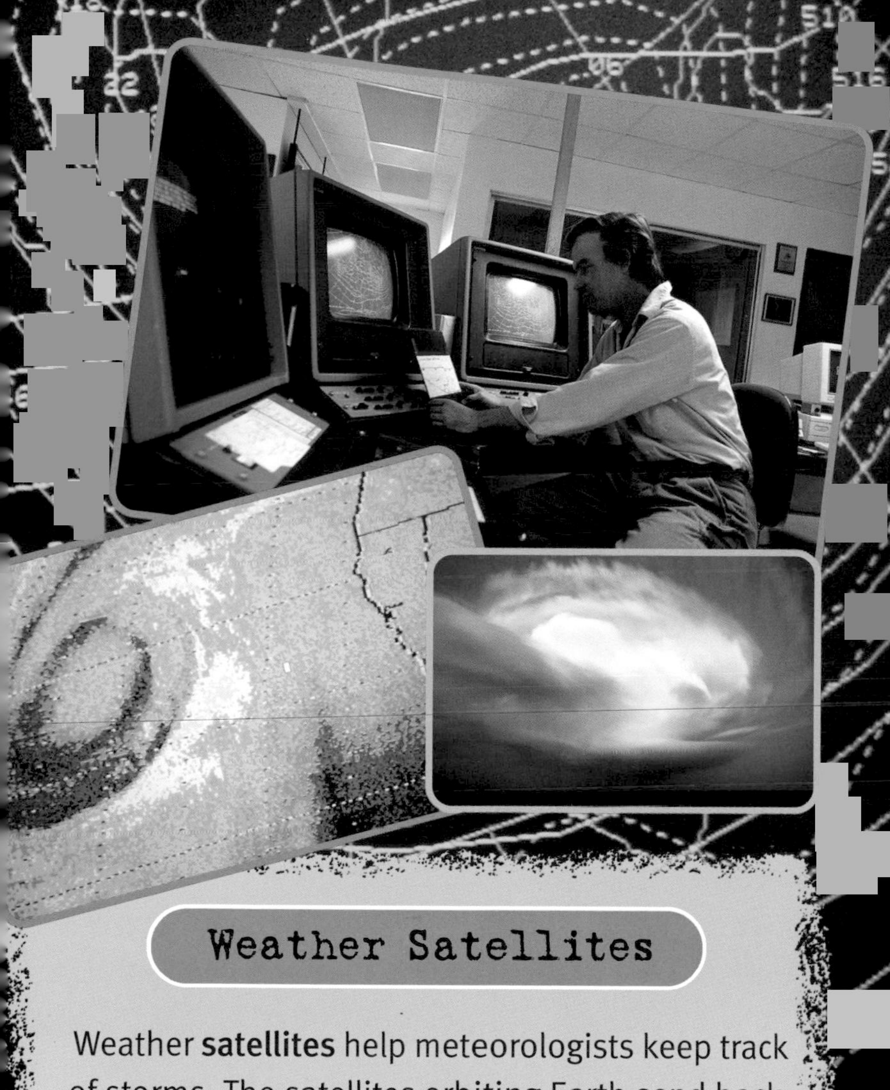

Weather Satellites

Weather **satellites** help meteorologists keep track of storms. The satellites orbiting Earth send back computer pictures of the atmosphere below. Meteorologists use these pictures to spot the supercell storms that can produce tornadoes.

Radar

Radar is an electronic device that is used to detect and locate objects. The word radar comes from **r**adio **d**etection **a**nd **r**anging. Radar can be used in lots of different ways. It is important to weather forecasters because it can detect rain and hail in clouds.

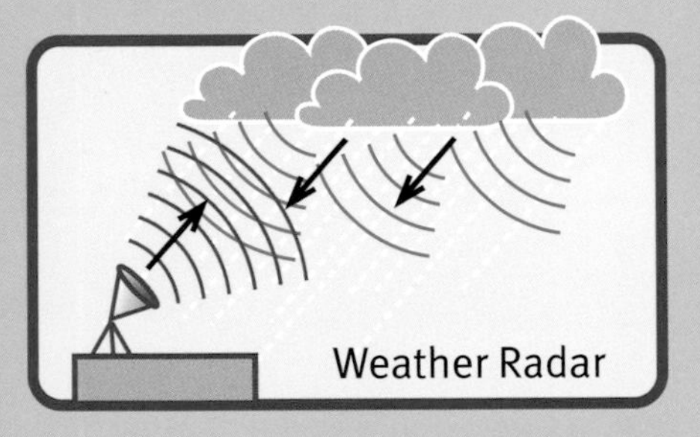

The radar sends out radio waves in all directions. When a wave hits raindrops, part of the signal bounces back to the radar. The amount of energy sent back and the amount of time it takes for the waves to return tell weather forecasters how much rain there is and how far away it is.

Doppler Radar

Although weather satellites can detect supercell storms, they cannot locate individual tornadoes. To do this, meteorologists use Doppler radar. Doppler radar works on the same principle as the Doppler effect.

THE DOPPLER EFFECT

When a train passes you sounding its horn, the note seems to change from high to low. This is the "Doppler effect."

When a train comes toward you, its speed added to the speed of the sound waves makes the sound waves that you hear "bunch up."
"Bunched-up" sound waves = higher frequency = higher note.

When a train is going away from you, the sound waves that you hear are stretched out.
"Stretched-out" sound waves = lower frequency = lower note.

Radar signals are sent into a storm cloud. When the signals show that one side of the storm is coming toward the radar while the other side is moving away, the scientists know that the cloud is rotating and may produce a tornado.

Doppler radar can only detect storms that are moving toward or away from it, not across it. Also, Doppler radar needs to be close to the storm to measure accurately how fast it is moving.

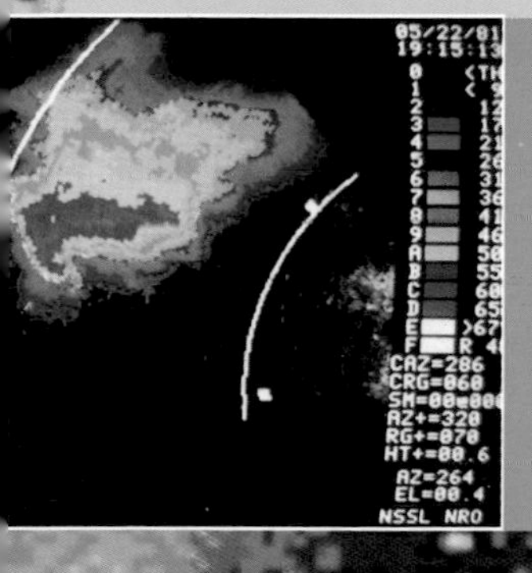

A Doppler radar screen – the different colors on the screen show the direction and speed of the wind. Red shows the fastest speed away from the radar. Yellow shows the fastest speed toward the radar.

Storm Chasers

Meteorologists chase tornadoes to try and learn more about them. There are other people who chase tornadoes just because they are fascinated by them. Some of these people volunteer to watch storms and pass any information about them to the National Weather Service. Radar can't always detect tornadoes, and so teams of storm spotters are needed to help keep track of storms and tornadoes.

The storm chasers are trained to recognize which weather conditions and storms may produce a tornado. Their knowledge and experience help keep them safe. The public are not encouraged to chase tornadoes – it's a risky activity. To spot a tornado, chasers must drive through gusting winds, driving rain, and large hailstones. A storm chaser will often get within a few miles of a tornado, which can be very dangerous.

There are professional storm chasers who will take passengers in their chase vehicles for a fee. They use computers and weather reports to try and find likely storms or tornadoes, and explain everything to their passengers as they go.

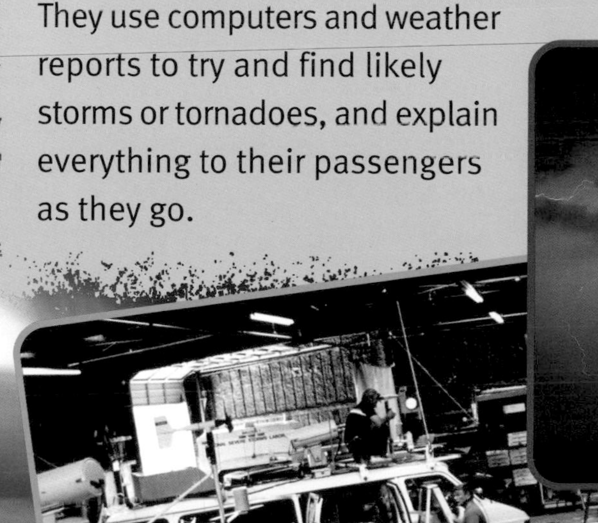

A Storm Chaser's Story

On 21 March 1991, David Gold, a professional storm chaser and meteorologist, was searching for tornadoes in Oklahoma with two other storm chasers. In the afternoon, they spotted a supercell. They drove under it and were pounded by large hailstones that were being blown by winds of up to 60 miles per hour. A quick weather check on the computer told them that the storm was moving away from them. So they changed direction and drove closer to where they thought the tornado might strike.

As the car approached the storm, the chasers noticed a powerful **rotation**. They knew that a tornado could be hidden in the heavy rain and hail. After driving into the storm, they saw a large tornado moving toward them. They drove out of its way – just seconds before it passed over the place where they'd been. David was able to videotape the tornado as it crossed the highway behind them.

The chasers took risks to spot the tornado, and they were lucky that day. Their close call has not stopped them from chasing tornadoes. They still hunt them, hoping to learn more about one of nature's most devastating occurrences.

5. Tornado Watch

Before World War II, there was no national network of tornado warnings in the United States. In the last fifty years, severe weather information has become more available and more accurate. Today, local radio and television stations can warn people of possible tornadoes by issuing tornado "watches" or "warnings."

Tornado Watch: Tornadoes are possible in the current conditions. Stay tuned to the radio or TV.

Tornado Warning: A tornado has been sighted. Take shelter immediately.

Spotting a Tornado

Tornadoes come in different sizes, shapes, and colors. Some are very wide and fat, reaching straight from ground to sky. Others are very thin and curvy. If it's raining heavily or dark outside, people might not see a tornado approaching, but they usually hear it.

Signs of Tornado Activity

Any of these signs could indicate that a tornado is coming:

- a sound that starts off like a waterfall and gets louder and louder like a freight train
- a strange calm or quiet during or immediately after a thunderstorm
- a greenish look outside
- a funnel cloud that appears brown or black, meaning it has reached the ground and is sucking up dirt
- a rotating cloud in the sky.

Tornado Safety

Tornadoes can strike very quickly. It's important that you know what to do *before* you find yourself in one.

- Know and understand your school's tornado drill – if there isn't one, ask the principal to make one.
- If a tornado happens while you are at school, follow your teacher's instructions.
- Keep calm, and move in an orderly way.
- Leave the gym, cafeteria, or auditorium – these large rooms may not be safe.
- Move to an interior room or hallway.
- Stay away from windows.
- Crouch down and cover your head with an object such as a cushion, or your hands.

Websites

To find out more about tornadoes, check out the following websites:

- National Weather Service – http://www.nws.noaa.gov
- The Weather Channel – http://www.weather.com
- Storm Prediction Center – http://www.spc.noaa.gov
- National Climatic Data Center – http://www.ncdc.noaa.gov
- National Severe Storms Laboratory – http://www.nssl.noaa.gov
- Silver Lining Tours – http://www.silverlining.pair.com
- Tornado Project Online – http://www.tornadoproject.com

Glossary

(These words are printed in bold type the first time they appear in the book.)

funnel cloud: a rotating column of air extending from the base of a thunderstorm but not in contact with the ground

humid: warm and moist

meteorologist: a scientist who studies weather

rotation: rapid circular movement

satellite: an information-gathering instrument that orbits Earth

supercell: a storm cloud that can produce a tornado

Index